Three Little Things

created by

Jules Chandler

Independently Published

ISBN: 9798562541710

I dedicate this book to my two girls.
I owe my existence to you.

"Every good and perfect thing is from above."
James 1:17

Olivia.
xx

Firstly, I apologise for the soppiness of the dedication.

My life has seen frequent pockets of deep darkness. If it wasn't for my children, I wouldn't be here. The kids are great for keeping me in the minute and helping me organise further than today, all at the same time. They fill me with love and they drive me nuts. And that's okay. That's their job. My job is to show up, be present, love them no matter what and stay calm. I have an army of tools to help me to attempt to carry this out and I use many of them on a daily basis.

My brain is not a naturally calm and happy one.

I'm sure some of you can resonate and I'm also sure some of you who have met me are saying "Whaaaat?? But you're so bubbly!".

Yep, I am. I am frequently a rather chipper soul, but I'm also blessed with a brain that doesn't make happy hormones easily.

I attempt to cultivate the balance of those happy hormones with a daily spiritual practice.

Part of that practice is short lists of things I am grateful for and this has been a part of my spiritual toolkit for nearly two decades.

So how does all this "short-list journaling" work? Well, when you write a gratitude list, you activate a positive filter in the brain and Hey Presto, you're seeing silver linings everywhere! It's that simple.

It's not the same as journaling which is an amazing tool if you get on with it, fabulous in fact. If however, like me, you find it overwhelming and get yourself into a "self-analysis paralysis" pickle, then short-list journaling may work better for you.

I call it short-list journaling because it's a journal using a short list. Again, it's that simple.

Setting a positive intention for the day by writing things down that I'm grateful for helps me to see the good more frequently in the most annoying/painful of situations. For example. if someone cuts me up on the road "they must be in a hurry". If someone jumps ahead of me in the queue, "they must need to be somewhere". Of course, I'm not a saint.

It doesn't *always* flip to the positive, yet 8 out of 10 times it does. And *that* is a good feeling.

Plus, what I've discovered is this, I've stopped holding onto all of that annoyance/pain that would chew up my peace for hours at a time.

Rather than chowing down on that little grudge over and over, ruminating on the "ar$e of a driver" or the "selfish bl**dy queue-jumper" for the rest of the day, I can put it to rest. When my head hits the pillow, I'm not thinking about how annoying they were. My brain is at peace and smiling!

How does this happen?

By the time I'm in bed, I've written the three little things that have lit my day up; a brief walk in the sunshine, a special offer online because I just made the cut-off date, dinner with my kids where no-one moaned and we all laughed. Simple stuff.

An Instagram follower commented that she used gratitude journaling before bed too and liked to think of her brain "marinading in positivity" as she slept. I love that image. My brain stewing in serenity as I sleep.

Bedtime routines often start in the morning and this routine is no different.

Writing down three little things that I am grateful for first thing in the morning, within a calm and quiet space, sets my intention and switches on the reticular activating system (RAS) in my brain (#nerdspeak for happy filter). This system then seeks out more happy incidences for me to notice as I go through my day. Capturing this at night as well is just sealing the deal for that ultimate positive-neuron-setting-sleep-marinade!

I am known to (annoyingly some might say!) encourage many of the people I know to harness this tool. I bang on and on about it because it is SO easy and is such a small amount of effort for such large gain. It's literally the ultimate "magic bullet" to change your mindset.

The only thing you have to do is turn up to the page and write down three sets of happy thoughts. One set in the morning, two sets in the evening.

Nine lines.

Each day.

And I mean write. No phones, no laptops, just you, a nice pen and paper. You've already made a positive decision to take up that challenge....you have this book in your hand. Yay! Go you!

Something spiritually beautiful and calming happens between the brain and the paper when we write.

The entire reason for creating this journal was to keep that process super simple. There are only these pages to read, the rest is up to you. Simple.

We are simple beings. But usually we have complex, tangled thought processes. T'is human nature.

Our clever little brains are frequently stuffed full of unrealistic belief systems that often aren't even our own! And many of us suffer with incessant, loud, critical voices telling us how rubbish we are. It can be exhausting.

So.......let's try to change that. Perhaps it will help those voices to become a little quieter. Our minds to become a little more still. A little peaceful even.

Please do aim to turn up here each day, morning and evening, to fill in the gaps provided for you. Along the way, maybe enjoy observing any subtle changes to your thinking patterns? Are you calmer? More tolerant?

This simple practice of gratitude has changed my thinking. It has enabled me to strengthen my "positivity muscle" and I can see the light in even the darkest of situations.

When our brains are activated in picking out gratitude, it will filter more of it into our day to day existence (remember that RAS). There is no situation where gratitude cannot be found. Not even the bad times.

I promise you.

Even when times are tough, as long as there is breath, there is life. And life is a gift to be grateful for.

Let's chat about how to write this thing...

Now, your list is *your* list. It can be short, long, detailed, one word, two words, a doodle even. It's your list. Write it your way. The first rule is, **it has to be positive**.

The second rule isn't actually a second rule.......it's an "encouraged option". **Mix it up**. Don't get stuck into too much of a routine. Some days write more, some less, some days write in capitals, some days lower case, some days loopy joined up grown-up writing, other days scribble down like a four year old. Maybe even draw out your tasks for that day? Play with it. Flex your creative muscles. Keep it fresh. Let your right brain (the creative side) have a little play.

There's a little extra room in the morning pages in case you fancy a doodle or you feel like extending your list that day to more things you're grateful for. No pressure.

There's also an extra page each day for general musings and reflections. Maybe extend on some of the points that you've listed, journal a bit, colour the shapes, do whatever comes to you. Some days you'll have time to do this, others you won't.

You may be thinking "Where do I even begin? How do I wake in the morning and jot down three things I'm happy and grateful about? What if I'm not grateful about anything?!"

T'is not easy to wake up full of the joys of spring, with perfect make-up on and birds tweeting at the window (Disney has *A Lot* to answer for, remember those imperfect ideals?!). Life is not ideal or perfect. Life is a challenge and some days you are likely to want to just lob the darn gratitude book across the room. These are the days when it is MOST helpful to use your short-list technique. It will help reset your mindset.

The positivity muscle is one we *learn* to build up just as it is when one goes to the gym to train our quads, lats, biceps, etc, (sidenote: those of you that *do* actually go to the gym regularly once you've paid your monthly fee....well done! Others, including myself....those intentions are *good* but we need to stop wasting our money and do some exercise we actually *enjoy*, like yoga or rollerskating or just walking fast!). We need to practice to build *all* new muscles including the mental ones. That's why it's called a practice and not a perfect #sorrythatonesabittwee

So again, let's clarify how to write this thing...

I suggest getting yourself a nice hot morning drink when you wake up, sit at the window, in a nice chair or up at the table or just go back to bed with a nice cuppa and this journal.

Watch your breathing for a few moments. And then prepare to list...what are you thankful for?

Once you've been at this a little while, you will see that every cloud does and can have a silver lining. Don't believe me? Here's some personal examples from some of my challenging times over the years...

Finding gratitude around a relationship breakdown:

- *Learning how I like to decorate my home (teal and mustard!).*
- *Learning who my true friends are.*
- *Knowing I will survive and that this situation won't kill me as it is temporary.*

OR

Hot coffee. Warm bed. It's Saturday.

<u>Finding gratitude around losing my baby</u>
<u>(impossible right? No...)</u>
- *I can get pregnant.*
- *Having the time to process my grief.*
- *Being able to see that I am not truly ready or well*
  enough to have another baby.

OR

2 hours sleep is better than nothing. Friends. Netflix.

<u>Gratitude around travelling through depression (again)</u>
- *Being able to stop and re-evaluate how I am living.*
- *Having conventional medication available.*
-*Realising (again) how amazing and supportive*
  the people around me are.

OR

I'm alive today. I only need to do today. I have gluten
free bread for toast (& it tastes okay!) and hot coffee.

Please realise that I am not saying that being grateful
means the situation is okay. This tool does not take
away the difficult times.

However, listing something positive about even a horrific situation may help to change mindset. It can sometimes make the difference between living and existing.

Personally speaking, picking out something, anything, positive in the darkest of times gives me more of an ability to stay afloat.

A little like holding onto a reed in a swamp...(for want of a better analogy!) it has stopped me from sinking deeper and enabled me to cling just for a bit when all I can do is cling. Just until the cavalry arrive and things start to pick up again. Life is obviously not tough all of the time and cultivating this "positivity muscle" as soon as you can will not only lift you a little each day but will ensure that it is firmly in place when the tough times do inevitably hit. #lifetrulyISarollercoasterthanksRonan

At the end of the day I write down three things that I enjoyed about my day, as I already mentioned earlier. I do this in bed, all snuggled and just before sleep. This again is simple: reading my magazine, seeing a friend (socially distanced of course), eating well today.

You may also have noticed on the page three extra little things....yip, I write down three things that I love about myself.

I know, I know. Its gross. It's hard. You don't like it........... yah yardy yah. I know how hard this one is to stomach and that many of you will balk at this. I used to. I had to get over it. And so will you. I promise.

Do you notice at all that we inhabit a world where it's become "uncool" to see and value how loved and lovable we all are? Think about it.

We are continually told by our world through the media that we are not good enough. But we ARE good enough just as we are.

And we are all enough. And we are all loved! Yes! You are good enough and loved. And SO lovable and SO loved. And SO enough! Yes you are. Yes YOU ARE! #stoparguing #yesyouare Okay I'll stop now.

It's a critical skill to love and value yourself. If we do not see our value, how can we rise above the lies of those over-critical inner voices that many of us consistently listen to?

It's often hard work to learn to write things you love about yourself. With this in mind, I've mixed it up a bit with different love lists each day to encourage the "self-love work" slowly if necessary.

When you hit a "Three little things that I love about me" section take a breath. Take a minute. Here's are some tips to help what may feel like a huge task of writing down things that you love about your unique and wonderful self? Let's start small...

I love..........
- my clothing choice today.
- that I cooked myself dinner.
- that I was kind to that annoying woman at work.

And then you're comfy with those external loves, you zone in more and get a little bit braver.....

I love......
- my thoughtfulness when I think about Christmas gifts.
- that I gave the last donut to a colleague at work. (don't make things up in your journal!).
- that I called my sister back after we had a fight and I apologised.

Then get a bit more targeted around your personality traits....the things about you that are just lovely...

I love.....
- my strength and tenacity.
- my humour and ability to make others laugh.
- my warm nature and approachability.

Wow, aren't you LUSH! See what you're doing here? You are building yourself up. It's sadly unlikely that anyone else is doing this important task for us at the moment so *why not* do it for ourselves? Go for it!

SO is this listing going to change your mentality overnight? No. But it's a fine start and a positive move forward in the right direction.

We all need to look after our mental health, especially in such challenging times. Whether we are mentally challenged or mentally peachy, it's a good idea to keep those reeds strong.

Positive mental attitudes are not a myth. Or something a bit "woo woo".

Positive Mental Attitudes are scientifically proven and a force to be reckoned with.

I'm passionate about building them and this is my prayer for you:

I pray that this simple journal will help you refine your mindset and experience the self-love that you are entitled to, that it will cultivate an awesome superpower within you, the phenomenal, powerful force of positivity, and bring light to your life in a whole new way.

Times are tough for us all right now.

In fact, I write this in my dressing gown at 1:42pm having not showered, cleaned my teeth or eaten anything but blueberry muffins (ssshhhhh, they were homemade and gluten free and made from oats and honey so it doesn't count).

Two weeks ago I was in the same (stinky!) position but debilitated in my bed, staring into space. That, however, was not my choice. I could not shower even if I'd wanted to. The life force had been sucked right out of me.

My mental health had completely broken down after a year of continual stress, trauma and the relentless "you know what" situation that we are experiencing worldwide. "Well how has that happened if you practice what you preach every day?!?" I hear you ask. "and why are you telling me this? Aren't you supposed to be some sorted practitioner who has it all together!!?"

No-one has it sorted or all together. Every day is a new day and a different day and we all have our stuff.

This listing technique doesn't stop the "bad stuff" happening, life is life after all. For me, these lists help me to travel through the bad times a little more easily and help me recover a little more quickly.

Throughout this latest spell of depression, I continued to list my gratitude and give thanks each day. Today I sit here at my laptop with my choices back in place due to some much-needed time off, the kicking in of conventional medication (no shame there anymore people, no shame, take the meds if you need to!) and the hope and positivity that this will soon be in the past and I shall be my usual cheery soul again.

This episode is already beginning to pass. Hopefully it'll pass quicker than a bingeworthy boxset on Netflix. In the meantime, I'll observe the flow of life as I firmly clutch to the strong reeds I have cultivated over the years.

Today I make the choice to sit here in my dressing gown (and I showered yesterday so I'm not *that* stinky!) driven by the desire to get this journal finished so that it can be available to *you* as soon as it possibly can be.

These lists, as simple as they are, hold me. They anchor me. They stop me drowning even in the smallest beginnings of darkness and they continue to keep me facing the light. In the easier times they fill me with subtle and abundant joy that flows from me into others.

I pray this journal reaches you just as you need it and that once you have made a beginning, it will help you in the same way that it continues to help me.
Off you pop then....

With love and gratitude,

Jules x

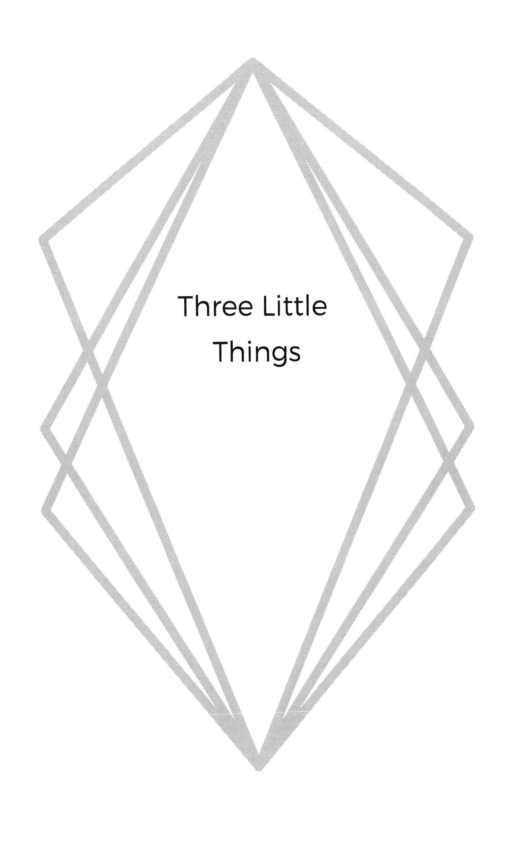

Three Little Things

Today's date:

Three things I am grateful for this morning:

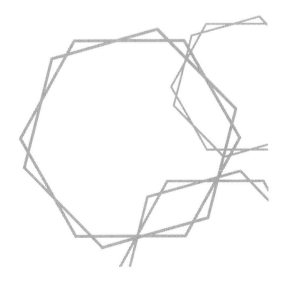

Today's date:

Three things I enjoyed about this day:

Three things I love about me:

Today's date:

General musings and reflections:

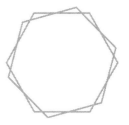

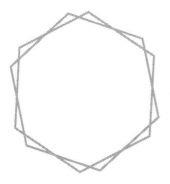

Today's date:

Three things I am grateful for this morning:

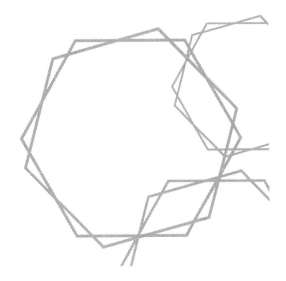

Today's date:

Three things I enjoyed about this day:

Three things I love about my life:

Today's date:

General musings and reflections:

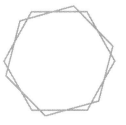

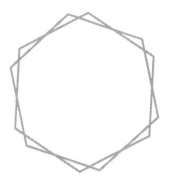

Today's date:

Three things I am grateful for this morning:

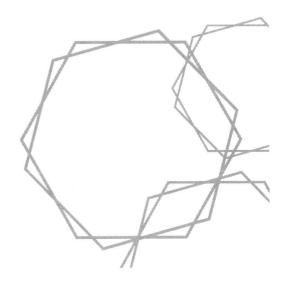

Today's date:

Three things I enjoyed about this day:

Three things I love about me:

Today's date:

General musings and reflections:

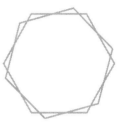

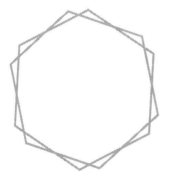

Today's date:

Three things I am grateful for this morning:

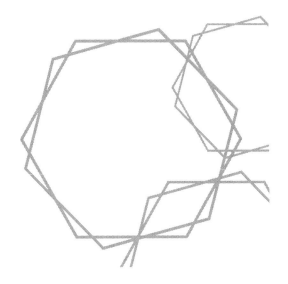

Today's date:

Three things I enjoyed about this day:

Three things I love about my living space:

Today's date:

General musings and reflections:

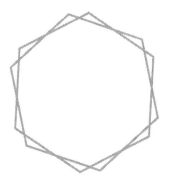

Today's date:

Three things I am grateful for this morning:

Today's date:

Three things I enjoyed about this day:

Three things I love about me:

Today's date:

General musings and reflections:

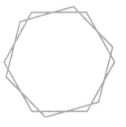

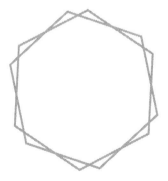

Today's date:

Three things I am grateful for this morning:

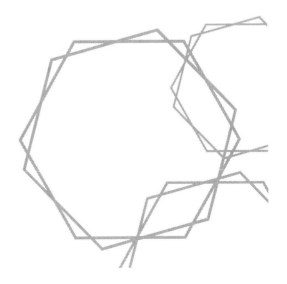

Today's date:

Three things I enjoyed about this day:

Three things I love about my family:

Today's date:

General musings and reflections:

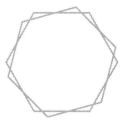

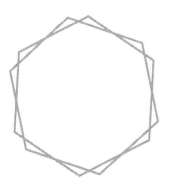

Today's date:

Three things I am grateful for this morning:

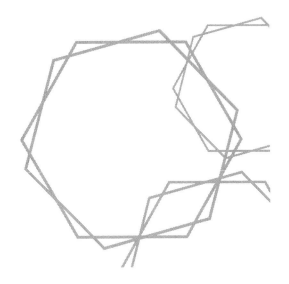

Today's date:

Three things I enjoyed about this day:

Three things I love about me:

Today's date:

General musings and reflections:

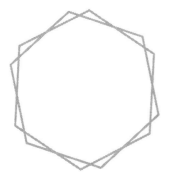

Today's date:

Three things I am grateful for this morning:

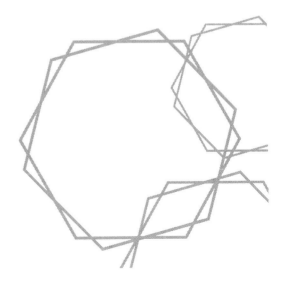

Today's date:

Three things I enjoyed about this day:

Three things I love about my skills:

Today's date:

General musings and reflections:

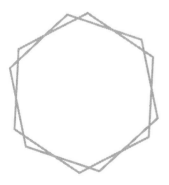

Today's date:

Three things I am grateful for this morning:

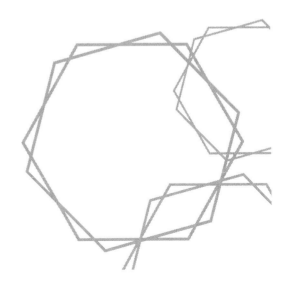

Today's date:

Three things I enjoyed about this day:

Three things I love about me:

Today's date:

General musings and reflections:

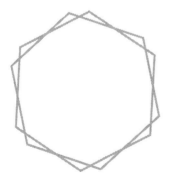

Today's date:

Three things I am grateful for this morning:

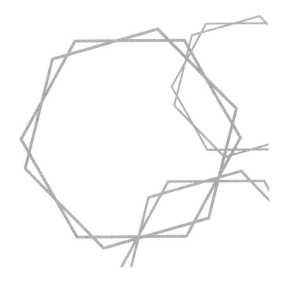

Today's date:

Three things I enjoyed about this day:

Three things I love about my character:

Today's date:

General musings and reflections:

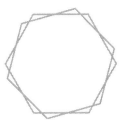

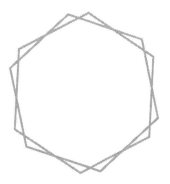

Today's date:

Three things I am grateful for this morning:

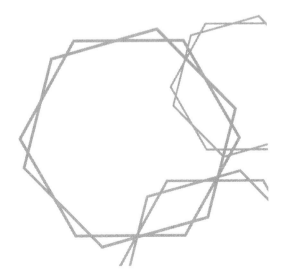

Today's date:

Three things I enjoyed about this day:

Three things I love about me:

Today's date:

General musings and reflections:

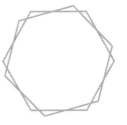

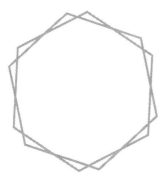

Today's date:

Three things I am grateful for this morning:

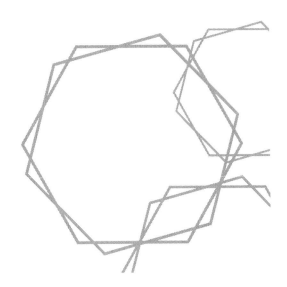

Today's date:

Three things I enjoyed about this day:

Three things I love about my body:

Today's date:

General musings and reflections:

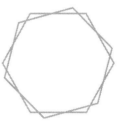

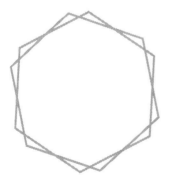

Today's date:

Three things I am grateful for this morning:

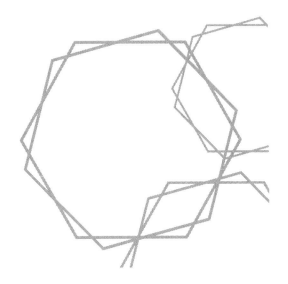

Today's date:

Three things I enjoyed about this day:

Three things I love about me:

Today's date:

General musings and reflections:

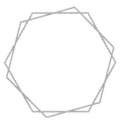

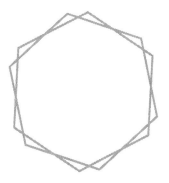

Today's date:

Three things I am grateful for this morning:

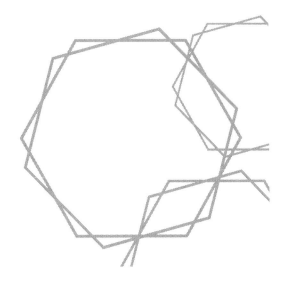

Today's date:

Three things I enjoyed about this day:

Three things I love about me:

Today's date:

General musings and reflections:

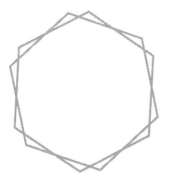

Today's date:

Three things I am grateful for this morning:

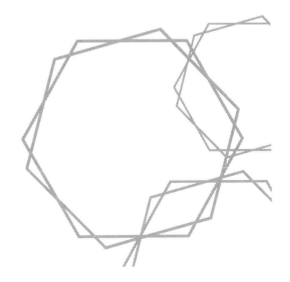

Today's date:

Three things I enjoyed about this day:

Three things I love about my life:

Today's date:

General musings and reflections:

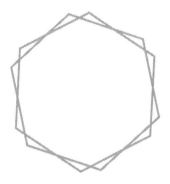

Today's date:

Three things I am grateful for this morning:

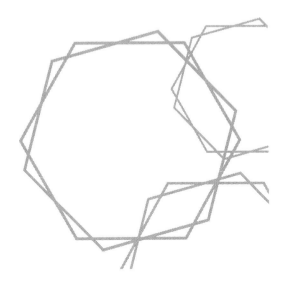

Today's date:

Three things I enjoyed about this day:

Three things I love about me:

Today's date:

General musings and reflections:

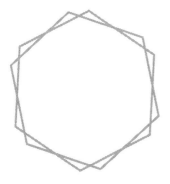

Today's date:

Three things I am grateful for this morning:

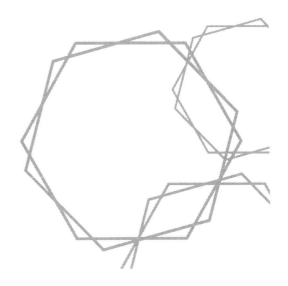

Today's date:

Three things I enjoyed about this day:

Three things I love about my living space:

Today's date:

General musings and reflections:

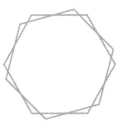

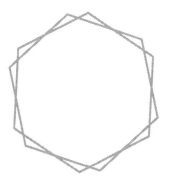

Today's date:

Three things I am grateful for this morning:

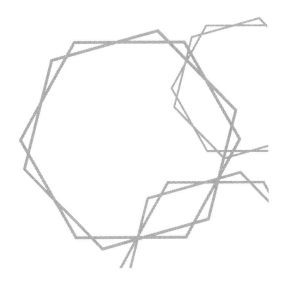

Today's date:

Three things I enjoyed about this day:

Three things I love about me:

Today's date:

General musings and reflections:

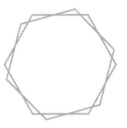

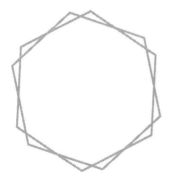

Today's date:

Three things I am grateful for this morning:

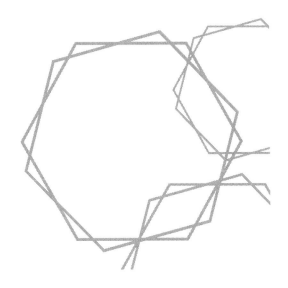

Today's date:

Three things I enjoyed about this day:

Three things I love about my family:

Today's date:

General musings and reflections:

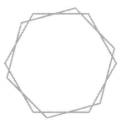

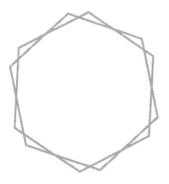

Today's date:

Three things I am grateful for this morning:

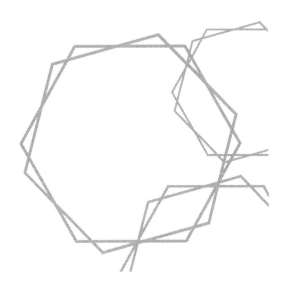

Today's date:

Three things I enjoyed about this day:

Three things I love about me:

Today's date:

General musings and reflections:

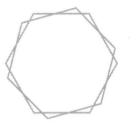

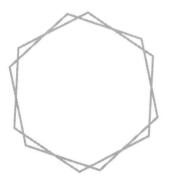

Today's date:

Three things I am grateful for this morning:

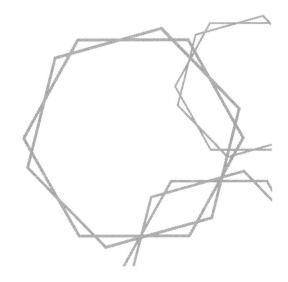

Today's date:

Three things I enjoyed about this day:

Three things I love about my skills:

Today's date:

General musings and reflections:

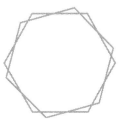

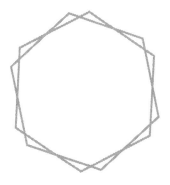

Today's date:

Three things I am grateful for this morning:

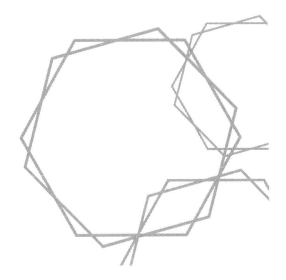

Today's date:

Three things I enjoyed about this day:

Three things I love about me:

Today's date:

General musings and reflections:

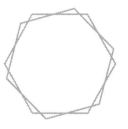

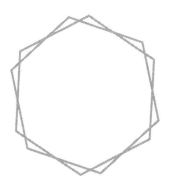

Today's date:

Three things I am grateful for this morning:

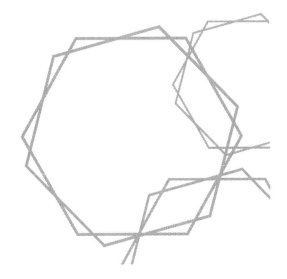

Today's date:

Three things I enjoyed about this day:

Three things I love about my character:

Today's date:

General musings and reflections:

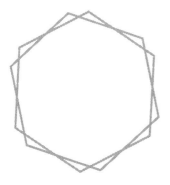

Today's date:

Three things I am grateful for this morning:

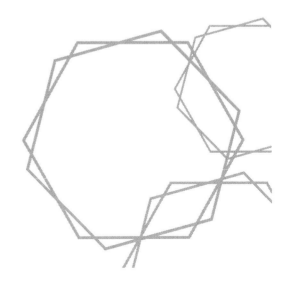

Today's date:

Three things I enjoyed about this day:

Three things I love about me:

Today's date:

General musings and reflections:

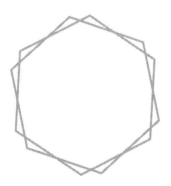

Today's date:

Three things I am grateful for this morning:

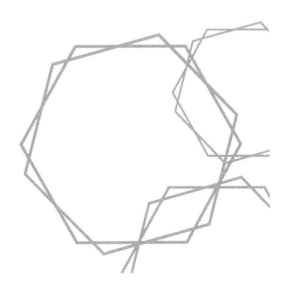

Today's date:

Three things I enjoyed about this day:

Three things I love about my body:

Today's date:

General musings and reflections:

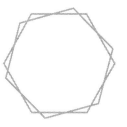

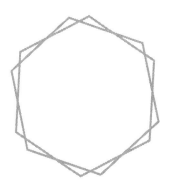

Today's date:

Three things I am grateful for this morning:

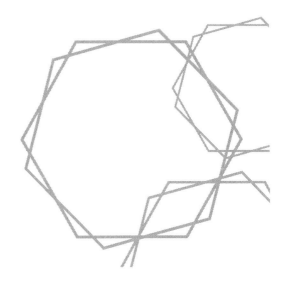

Today's date:

Three things I enjoyed about this day:

Three things I love about me:

Today's date:

General musings and reflections:

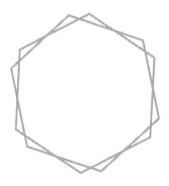

Today's date:

Three things I am grateful for this morning:

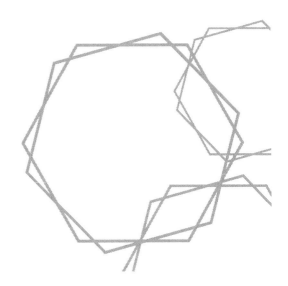

Today's date:

Three things I enjoyed about this day:

Three things I love about me:

Today's date:

General musings and reflections:

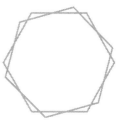

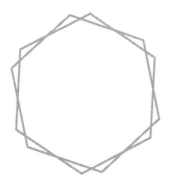

Today's date:

Three things I am grateful for this morning:

Today's date:

Three things I enjoyed about this day:

- -

- -

- -

Three things I love about my life:

- -

- -

- -

Today's date:

General musings and reflections:

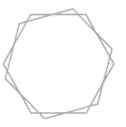

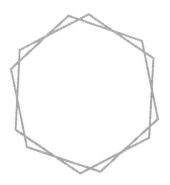

Today's date:

Three things I am grateful for this morning:

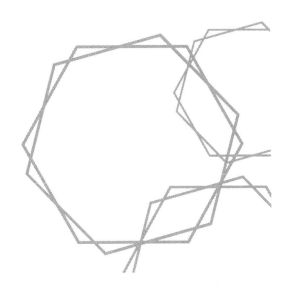

Today's date:

Three things I enjoyed about this day:

Three things I love about me:

Today's date:

General musings and reflections:

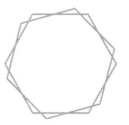

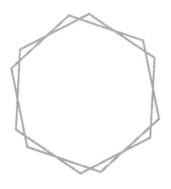

Today's date:

Three things I am grateful for this morning:

Today's date:

Three things I enjoyed about this day:

Three things I love about my living space:

Today's date:

General musings and reflections:

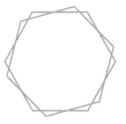

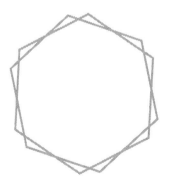

Today's date:

Three things I am grateful for this morning:

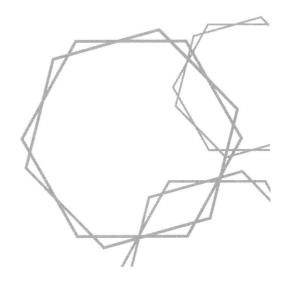

Today's date:

Three things I enjoyed about this day:

Three things I love about me:

Today's date:

General musings and reflections:

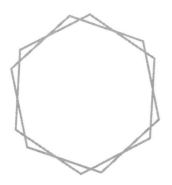

Today's date:

Three things I am grateful for this morning:

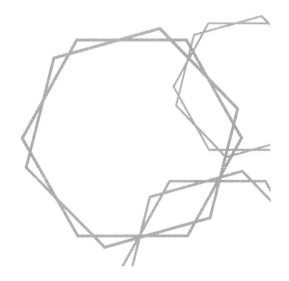

Today's date:

Three things I enjoyed about this day:

Three things I love about my family:

Today's date:

General musings and reflections:

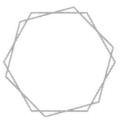

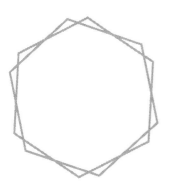

Today's date:

Three things I am grateful for this morning:

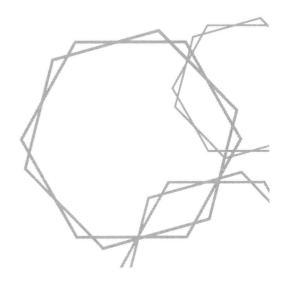

Today's date:

Three things I enjoyed about this day:

Three things I love about me:

Today's date:

General musings and reflections:

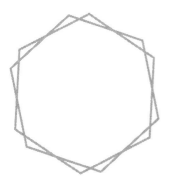

Today's date:

Three things I am grateful for this morning:

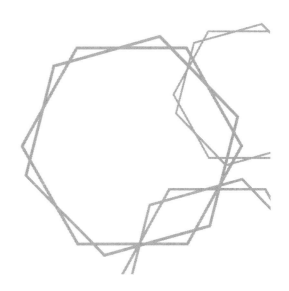

Today's date:

Three things I enjoyed about this day:

Three things I love about my skills:

Today's date:

General musings and reflections:

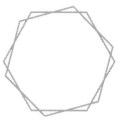

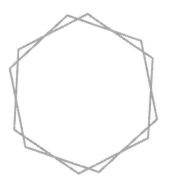

Today's date:

Three things I am grateful for this morning:

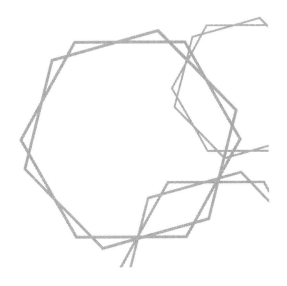

Today's date:

Three things I enjoyed about this day:

Three things I love about me:

Today's date:

General musings and reflections:

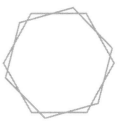

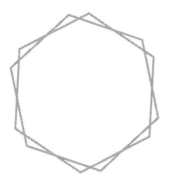

Today's date:

Three things I am grateful for this morning:

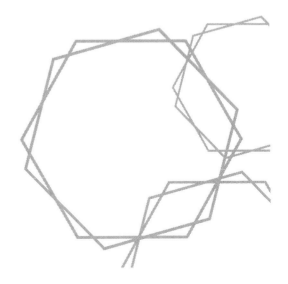

Today's date:

Three things I enjoyed about this day:

Three things I love about my character:

Today's date:

General musings and reflections:

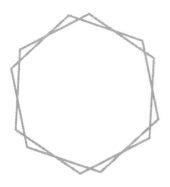

Today's date:

Three things I am grateful for this morning:

Today's date:

Three things I enjoyed about this day:

Three things I love about me:

Today's date:

General musings and reflections:

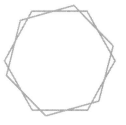

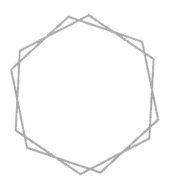

Today's date:

Three things I am grateful for this morning:

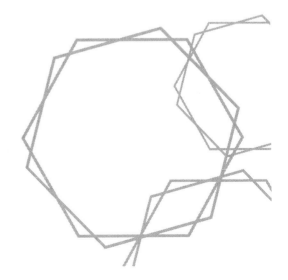

Today's date:

Three things I enjoyed about this day:

Three things I love about my body:

Today's date:

General musings and reflections:

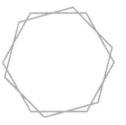

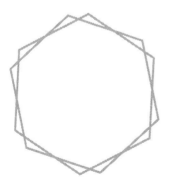

Today's date:

Three things I am grateful for this morning:

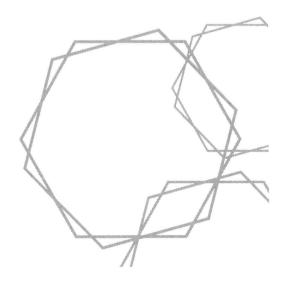

Today's date:

Three things I enjoyed about this day:

Three things I love about me:

Today's date:

General musings and reflections:

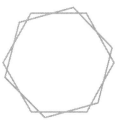

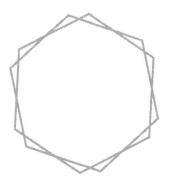

Today's date:

Three things I am grateful for this morning:

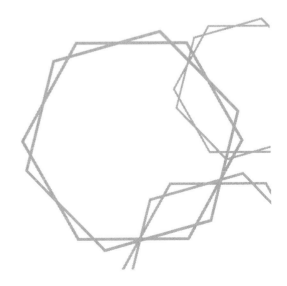

Today's date:

Three things I enjoyed about this day:

Three things I love about me:

Today's date:

General musings and reflections:

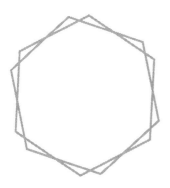

Today's date:

Three things I am grateful for this morning:

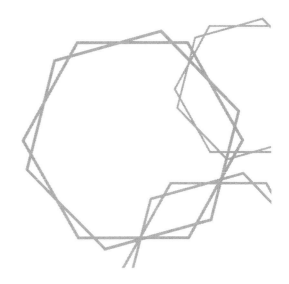

Today's date:

Three things I enjoyed about this day:

Three things I love about my life:

Today's date:

General musings and reflections:

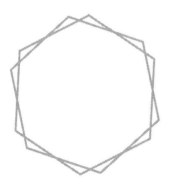

Today's date:

Three things I am grateful for this morning:

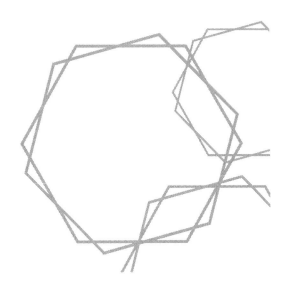

Today's date:

Three things I enjoyed about this day:

Three things I love about me:

Today's date:

General musings and reflections:

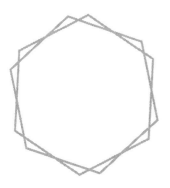

Today's date:

Three things I am grateful for this morning:

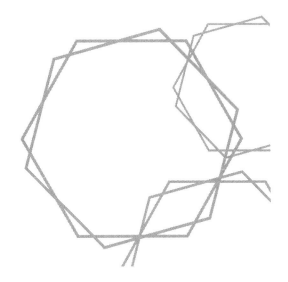

Today's date:

Three things I enjoyed about this day:

Three things I love about my living space:

Today's date:

General musings and reflections:

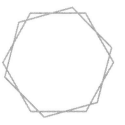

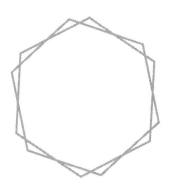

Today's date:

Three things I am grateful for this morning:

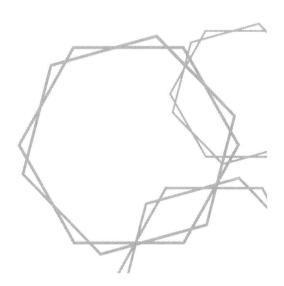

Today's date:

Three things I enjoyed about this day:

Three things I love about me:

Today's date:

General musings and reflections:

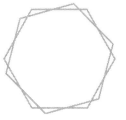

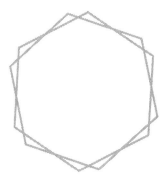

Today's date:

Three things I am grateful for this morning:

Today's date:

Three things I enjoyed about this day:

Three things I love about my family:

Today's date:

General musings and reflections:

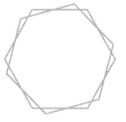

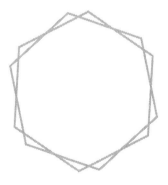

Today's date:

Three things I am grateful for this morning:

Today's date:

Three things I enjoyed about this day:

Three things I love about me:

Today's date:

General musings and reflections:

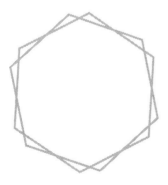

Today's date:

Three things I am grateful for this morning:

Today's date:

Three things I enjoyed about this day:

Three things I love about my skills:

Today's date:

General musings and reflections:

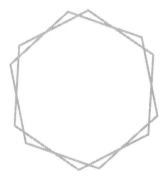

Today's date:

Three things I am grateful for this morning:

Today's date:

Three things I enjoyed about this day:

Three things I love about me:

Today's date:

General musings and reflections:

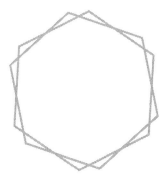

Today's date:

Three things I am grateful for this morning:

Today's date:

Three things I enjoyed about this day:

Three things I love about my character:

Today's date:

General musings and reflections:

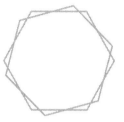

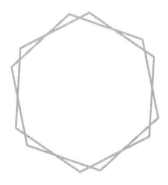

Today's date:

Three things I am grateful for this morning:

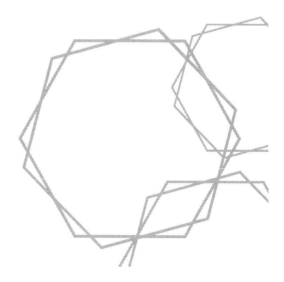

Today's date:

Three things I enjoyed about this day:

Three things I love about me:

Today's date:

General musings and reflections:

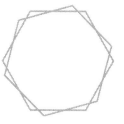

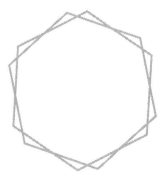

Today's date:

Three things I am grateful for this morning:

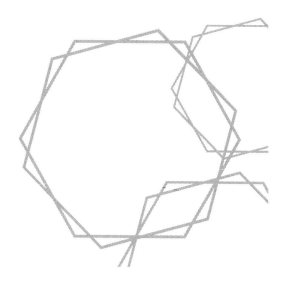

Today's date:

Three things I enjoyed about this day:

Three things I love about my body:

Today's date:

General musings and reflections:

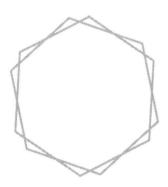

Today's date:

Three things I am grateful for this morning:

\--

\--

\--

Today's date:

Three things I enjoyed about this day:

Three things I love about me:

Today's date:

General musings and reflections:

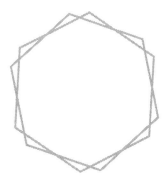

Today's date:

Three things I am grateful for this morning:

Today's date:

Three things I enjoyed about this day:

Three things I love about me:

Today's date:

General musings and reflections:

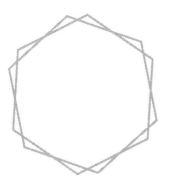

Today's date:

Three things I am grateful for this morning:

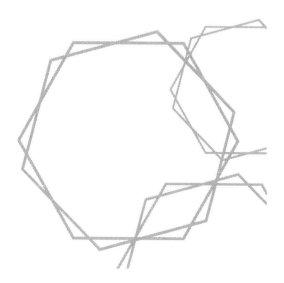

Today's date:

Three things I enjoyed about this day:

_____

_____

_____

Three things I love about my life:

_____

_____

_____

Today's date:

General musings and reflections:

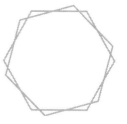

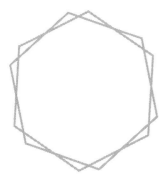

Today's date:

Three things I am grateful for this morning:

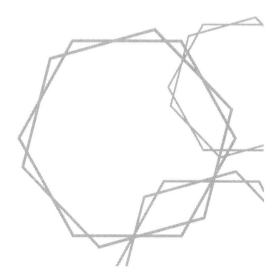

Today's date:

Three things I enjoyed about this day:

Three things I love about me:

Today's date:

General musings and reflections:

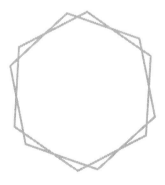

Today's date:

Three things I am grateful for this morning:

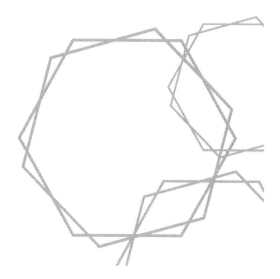

Today's date:

Three things I enjoyed about this day:

_____

_____

_____

Three things I love about my living space:

_____

_____

_____

Today's date:

General musings and reflections:

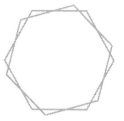

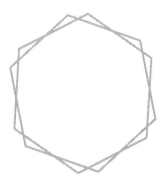

Today's date:

Three things I am grateful for this morning:

Today's date:

Three things I enjoyed about this day:

Three things I love about me:

Today's date:

General musings and reflections:

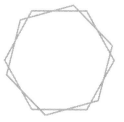

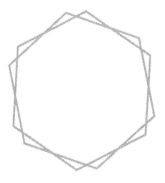

Today's date:

Three things I am grateful for this morning:

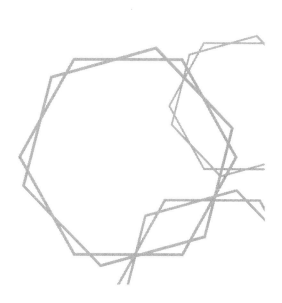

Today's date:

Three things I enjoyed about this day:

Three things I love about my family:

Today's date:

General musings and reflections:

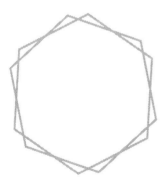

Today's date:

Three things I am grateful for this morning:

Today's date:

Three things I enjoyed about this day:

Three things I love about me:

Today's date:

General musings and reflections:

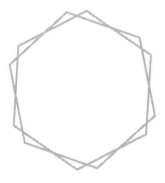

Today's date:

Three things I am grateful for this morning:

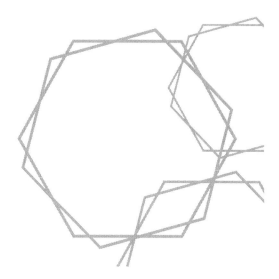

Today's date:

Three things I enjoyed about this day:

Three things I love about my skills:

Today's date:

General musings and reflections:

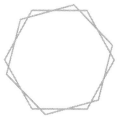

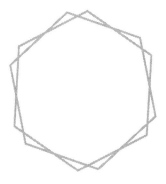

Today's date:

Three things I am grateful for this morning:

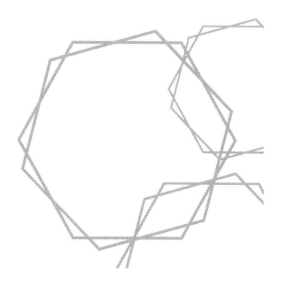

Today's date:

Three things I enjoyed about this day:

Three things I love about me:

Today's date:

General musings and reflections:

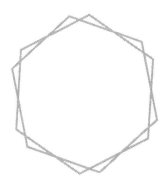

Today's date:

Three things I am grateful for this morning:

Today's date:

Three things I enjoyed about this day:

Three things I love about my character:

Today's date:

General musings and reflections:

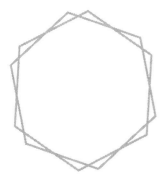

Today's date:

Three things I am grateful for this morning:

Today's date:

Three things I enjoyed about this day:

Three things I love about me:

Today's date:

General musings and reflections:

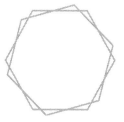

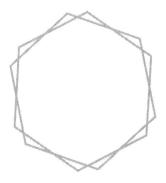

Today's date:

Three things I am grateful for this morning:

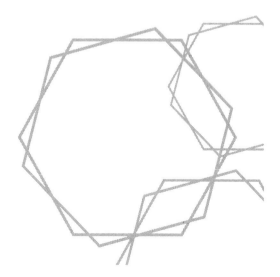

Today's date:

Three things I enjoyed about this day:

Three things I love about my body:

Today's date:

General musings and reflections:

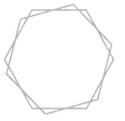

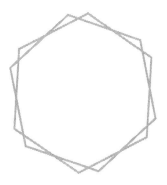

Today's date:

Three things I am grateful for this morning:

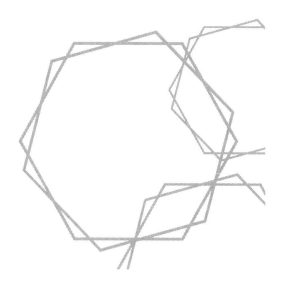

Today's date:

Three things I enjoyed about this day:

Three things I love about me:

Today's date:

General musings and reflections:

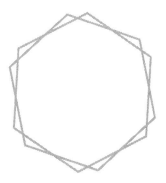

Today's date:

Three things I am grateful for this morning:

Today's date:

Three things I enjoyed about this day:

Three things I love about me:

Today's date:

General musings and reflections:

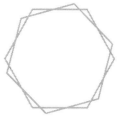

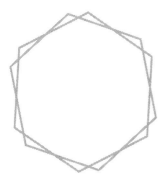

Today's date:

Three things I am grateful for this morning:

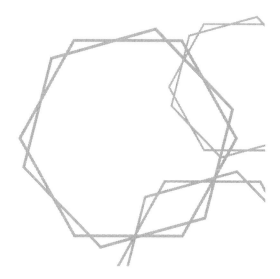

Today's date:

Three things I enjoyed about this day:

Three things I love about my life:

Today's date:

General musings and reflections:

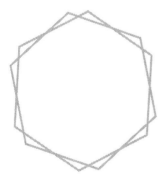

Today's date:

Three things I am grateful for this morning:

\-

\-

\-

Today's date:

Three things I enjoyed about this day:

Three things I love about me:

Today's date:

General musings and reflections:

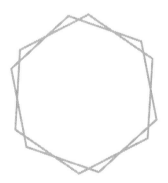

Today's date:

Three things I am grateful for this morning:

Today's date:

Three things I enjoyed about this day:

Three things I love about my living space:

Today's date:

General musings and reflections:

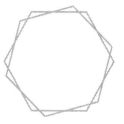

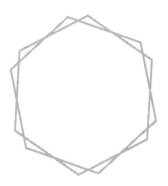

Today's date:

Three things I am grateful for this morning:

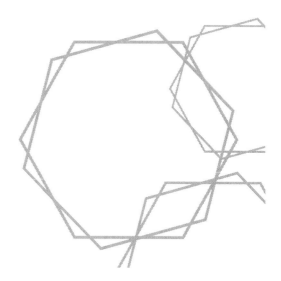

Today's date:

Three things I enjoyed about this day:

Three things I love about me:

Today's date:

General musings and reflections:

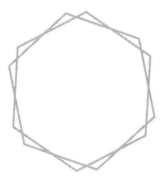

Today's date:

Three things I am grateful for this morning:

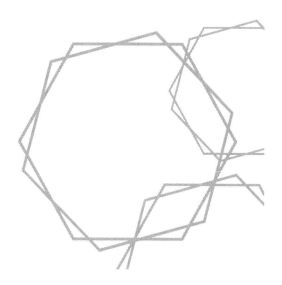

Today's date:

Three things I enjoyed about this day:

Three things I love about my family:

Today's date:

General musings and reflections:

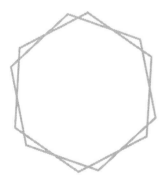

Today's date:

Three things I am grateful for this morning:

Today's date:

Three things I enjoyed about this day:

Three things I love about me:

Today's date:

General musings and reflections:

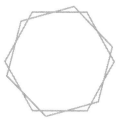

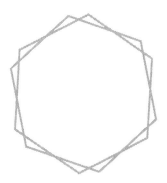

Today's date:

Three things I am grateful for this morning:

Today's date:

Three things I enjoyed about this day:

Three things I love about my skills:

Today's date:

General musings and reflections:

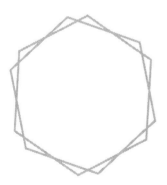

Today's date:

Three things I am grateful for this morning:

Today's date:

Three things I enjoyed about this day:

Three things I love about me:

Today's date:

General musings and reflections:

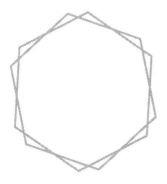

Today's date:

Three things I am grateful for this morning:

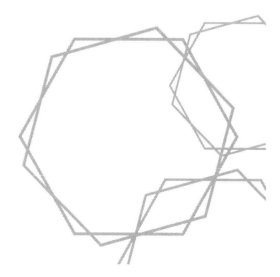

Today's date:

Three things I enjoyed about this day:

Three things I love about my character:

Today's date:

General musings and reflections:

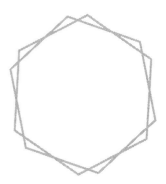

Today's date:

Three things I am grateful for this morning:

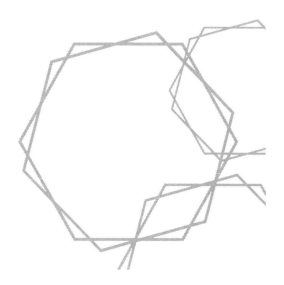

Today's date:

Three things I enjoyed about this day:

Three things I love about me:

Today's date:

General musings and reflections:

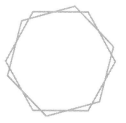

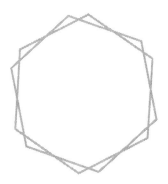

Today's date:

Three things I am grateful for this morning:

Today's date:

Three things I enjoyed about this day:

Three things I love about my body:

Today's date:

General musings and reflections:

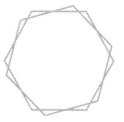

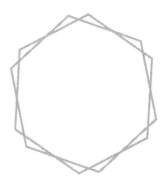

Today's date:

Three things I am grateful for this morning:

Today's date:

Three things I enjoyed about this day:

Three things I love about me:

Today's date:

General musings and reflections:

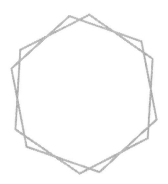

Today's date:

Three things I am grateful for this morning:

Today's date:

Three things I enjoyed about this day:

Three things I love about me:

Today's date:

General musings and reflections:

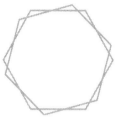

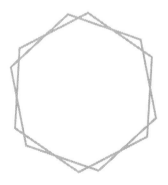

Today's date:

Three things I am grateful for this morning:

Today's date:

Three things I enjoyed about this day:

\---

\---

\---

Three things I love about my life:

\---

\---

\---

Today's date:

General musings and reflections:

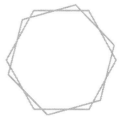

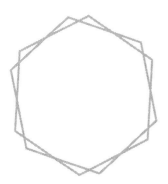

Today's date:

Three things I am grateful for this morning:

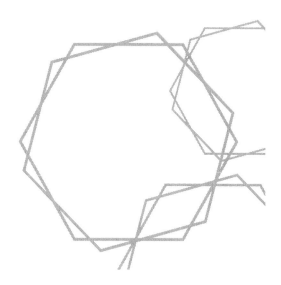

Today's date:

Three things I enjoyed about this day:

Three things I love about me:

Today's date:

General musings and reflections:

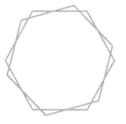

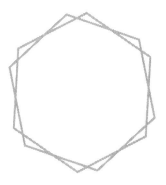

Today's date:

Three things I am grateful for this morning:

Today's date:

Three things I enjoyed about this day:

Three things I love about my living space:

Today's date:

General musings and reflections:

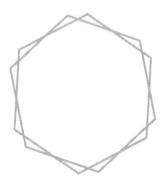

Today's date:

Three things I am grateful for this morning:

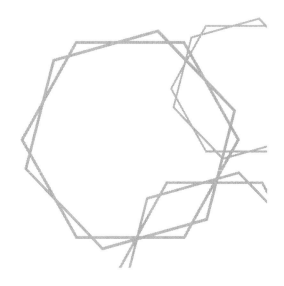

Today's date:

Three things I enjoyed about this day:

Three things I love about me:

Today's date:

General musings and reflections:

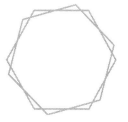

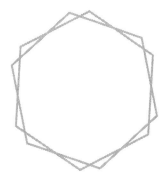

Today's date:

Three things I am grateful for this morning:

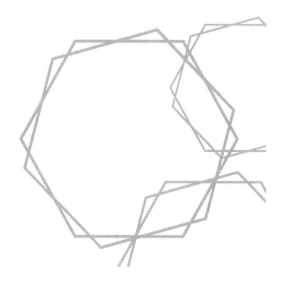

Today's date:

Three things I enjoyed about this day:

Three things I love about my family:

Today's date:

General musings and reflections:

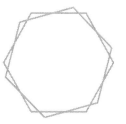

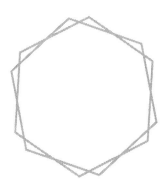

Today's date:

Three things I am grateful for this morning:

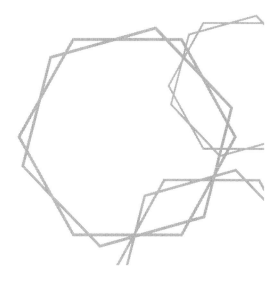

Today's date:

Three things I enjoyed about this day:

Three things I love about me:

Today's date:

General musings and reflections:

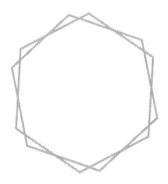

Today's date:

Three things I am grateful for this morning:

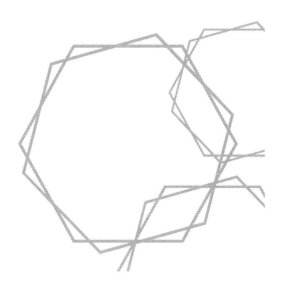

Today's date:

Three things I enjoyed about this day:

Three things I love about my skills:

Today's date:

General musings and reflections:

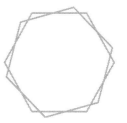

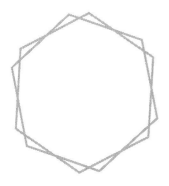

Today's date:

Three things I am grateful for this morning:

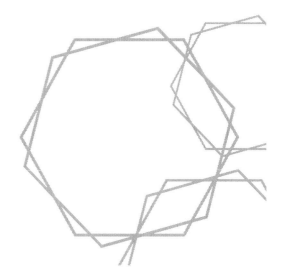

Today's date:

Three things I enjoyed about this day:

Three things I love about me:

Today's date:

General musings and reflections:

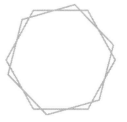

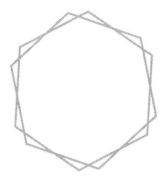

Today's date:

Three things I am grateful for this morning:

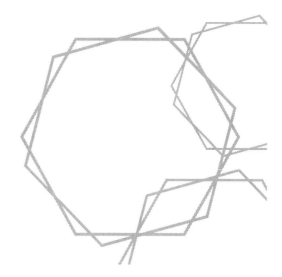

Today's date:

Three things I enjoyed about this day:

Three things I love about my character:

Today's date:

General musings and reflections:

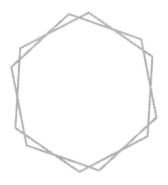

Today's date:

Three things I am grateful for this morning:

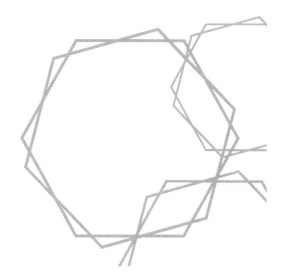

Today's date:

Three things I enjoyed about this day:

Three things I love about me:

Today's date:

General musings and reflections:

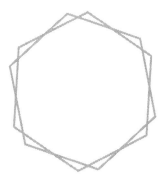

Today's date:

Three things I am grateful for this morning:

\---

\---

\---

Today's date:

Three things I enjoyed about this day:

Three things I love about my body:

Today's date:

General musings and reflections:

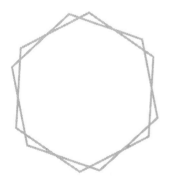

Today's date:

Three things I am grateful for this morning:

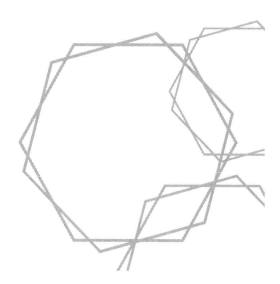

Today's date:

Three things I enjoyed about this day:

Three things I love about me:

Today's date:

General musings and reflections:

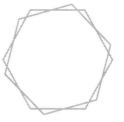

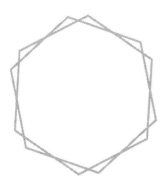